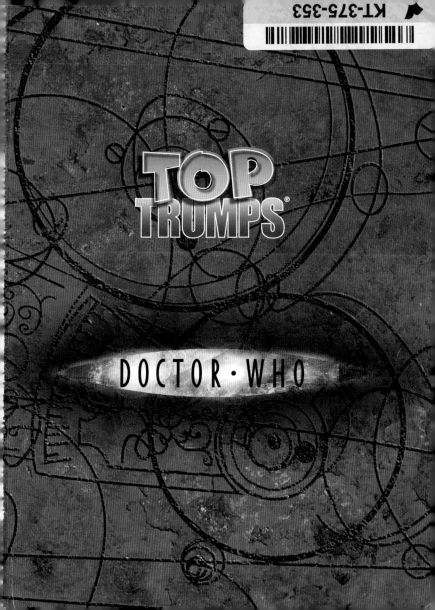

TOP TRUMPS

DOCTOR·WHO

This book is officially licensed by Winning Moves UK Ltd, owners of the Top Trumps registered trademark.

BBC, DOCTOR WHO (word marks, logos and devices), TARDIS, DALEKS, CYBERMAN and K-9 (word marks and devices) are trade marks of the British Broadcasting Corporation and are used under licence.

BBC logo © BBC 1996. Doctor Who logo © BBC 2004. Tardis image © BBC 1963. Dalek image © BBC/Terry Nation 1963. Cyberman image © BBC/Kit Pedlar/Gerry Davis 1963. K-9 image © BBC/Bob Baker/Dave Martin 1963. Licensed by BBC Worldwide Limited.

Moray Laing has asserted his right to be identified as the author of this book.

British Library Cataloguing-in-Publication Data:
A catalogue record for this book is available from the British Library

ISBN 978 1 84425 488 0

Library of Congress catalog card no. 2007934587

Published by Haynes Publishing,
Sparkford, Yeovil, Somerset BA22 7JJ, UK
Tel: +44 (0)1963 442030 Fax: +44 (0)1963 440001
Email: sales@haynes.co.uk Website: www.haynes.co.uk

Haynes North America, Inc.,
861 Lawrence Drive, Newbury Park, California 91320, USA

Printed and bound in Great Britain by J. H. Haynes & Co. Ltd, Sparkford

The Author

Moray Laing is the Editor of *Doctor Who Adventures* magazine. *Doctor Who* has followed him everywhere since he was three years old. He also wrote the first *Top Trumps Doctor Who* book in 2006.

TOP TRUMPS®

DOCTOR · WHO

Series Three

Contents

About
Top Trumps

It's now more than 30 years since Britain's kids first caught the Top Trumps craze. The game remained hugely popular until the 1990s, when it slowly drifted into obscurity. Then, in 1999, UK games company Winning Moves discovered it, bought it, dusted it down, gave it a thorough makeover and introduced it to a whole new generation. And so the Top Trumps legend continues.

Nowadays, there are Top Trumps titles for just about everyone, with subjects about animals, cars, ships, aircraft and all the great films and TV shows. Top Trumps is now even more popular than before. In Britain, a pack of Top Trumps is bought every six seconds! And it's not just British children who love the game. Children in Australasia, the Far East, the Middle East, all over Europe and in North America can buy Top Trumps at their local shops.

Today you can even play the game on the internet, interactive DVD, your games console and even your mobile phone.

You've played the game...

Now read the book!

**Haynes Publishing and Top Trumps have teamed
up to bring you this exciting new Top Trumps book,
in which you will find even more pictures, details
and statistics.**

**Top Trumps: Doctor Who features 45 key
characters from the third series of the hugely
successful television show, from the Doctor and
Martha to Dalek-Humans, Weeping Angels and, of
course, the Master. Packed with stunning pictures,
fascinating facts and all the vital statistics, this is
the essential pocket guide.**

**Look out for other Top Trumps books from Haynes
Publishing – even more facts, even more fun!**

The Doctor
Adventurer in time and space

The Doctor
Adventurer in time and space

The Doctor is a Time Lord who is over 900 years old. He travels in time and space in his fantastic ship called the TARDIS, which is disguised as a blue Earth police box. He has two hearts and is able to change his body whenever it becomes old or damaged. This handy Time Lord trick is a way of cheating death and is called regeneration. The Doctor has regenerated nine times so far and is currently in his tenth body. His people and home planet were destroyed during a hideous Time War with the Daleks – however, when he ends up on a planet at the end of the universe, he discovers that another Time Lord, his old enemy the Master, has also survived. Over the centuries the Doctor has fought all kinds of evil and injustice – and he always knows what to do when things get difficult and dangerous.

Statistics

DEBUT	Tenth Doctor first appeared in *The Parting of the Ways* (2005)
PLAYED BY	David Tennant (as the Tenth Doctor)
HOME	Gallifrey
STATUS	Friend
HEIGHT	1.85m
SCARE RATING	[2] Not applicable — unless he's very angry
SPECIAL FEATURES	[10] Two hearts, ability to regenerate
WEAPONS	[2] None barring intelligence and a sonic screwdriver
LIKES	Adventures in time and space, battling evil
DISLIKES	Monsters, injustice
TALK	'I'm not just a Time Lord, I'm the last of the Time Lords.'

Martha Jones
Medical student turned adventurer

Martha Jones

Medical student turned adventurer

Martha Jones is a 23-year-old medical student. Training to be a doctor at the Royal Hope Hospital when she first bumps into the Doctor, her hospital is at the centre of a Judoon mission to track down an alien – and Martha suddenly finds herself transported to the Moon. Brave and calm, the Doctor notices Martha's ability to adapt to dangerous situations as soon as he meets her – and as a reward for saving his life, he offers her one trip in the TARDIS. That one trip becomes a series of exciting adventures before the Doctor admits she is much more than just a passenger, and gives her a key to the TARDIS and a phone with universal roaming. Martha loves the Doctor, but finds it difficult living with his sadness at losing Rose. After saving the Earth from the Master, Martha decides to leave the TARDIS but tells the Doctor he must come back if she needs him.

Statistics

DEBUT	*Smith and Jones* (2007)
PLAYED BY	Freema Agyeman
HOME	London, England
STATUS	Fellow time traveller and friend
HEIGHT	1.53m
SCARE RATING	[1] Not applicable
SPECIAL FEATURES	[8] Medically trained, loyal, intelligent, brave
WEAPONS	[1] Not applicable
LIKES	The Doctor, adventures in time and space, helping others
DISLIKES	Going unnoticed by the Doctor, being treated as a TARDIS passenger
TALK	'I've seen worse, I've done the late shift in A&E.'

Donna Noble
Runaway bride

Donna Noble
Runaway bride

Donna Noble is about to marry Lance Bennett when she is transported into the TARDIS, much to the Doctor's surprise. At first Donna thinks she has been kidnapped, blaming her friend Nerys before the bossy bride discovers she is really at the centre of an alien plot. While the Doctor tries to get Donna to her wedding on time, Roboform mercenaries track her down and attempt to take her to the Empress of the Racnoss. Working for the Empress, Donna's fiancé has been dosing her with Huon particles in order to wake millions of hibernating Racnoss, horrific creatures that are waiting at the centre of the Earth. It takes Donna a while to trust the Doctor – at first she thinks he is from Mars – but together they defeat the Racnoss threat. The Doctor asks her to travel with him, but she decides his life is too frightening for her and watches him leave.

Statistics

DEBUT	*The Runaway Bride* (2006)
PLAYED BY	Catherine Tate
HOME	London, England
STATUS	Friend
HEIGHT	1.73m
SCARE RATING	[2] Harmless — but has a quick temper
SPECIAL FEATURES	[5] For a time Donna is filled with Huon particles
WEAPONS	[1] Not applicable
LIKES	Shouting
DISLIKES	Danger, Christmas
TALK	'Leave me alone. I just want to get married.'

Captain Jack Harkness
Immortal Time Agent

Captain Jack Harkness
Immortal Time Agent

Captain Jack Harkness comes from the 51st century – and is a long way from home when he tries to sell the Doctor and Rose a crashed spaceship in 1940s London. A former Time Agent, he woke up one morning and found that the agents had stolen memory of two years of his life. The reasons for this are unknown. Jack is exterminated by the Daleks, but is brought back to life by Rose when she has the power of the Vortex running through her. He heads back to Earth on his own using his Vortex Manipulator and is stranded there when the device breaks. Jack meets the Doctor and Martha when the TARDIS is refuelling in Cardiff. Although Jack can age, he is now unable to die, and interestingly, when he first became a Time Agent his nickname was the Face of Boe...

Statistics

DEBUT	*The Empty Child* (2005)
PLAYED BY	John Barrowman
HOME	Originally from the Boeshane Peninsula, now lives in Cardiff, Wales
STATUS	Friend
HEIGHT	1.85m
SCARE RATING	[2] Sometimes aggressive
SPECIAL FEATURES	[9] Loads of alien tech, the ability to live forever
WEAPONS	[5] Sonic blaster
LIKES	Flirting
DISLIKES	Cowards
TALK	'I was facing three Daleks. Death by extermination. And then I came back to life. What happened?'

Francine Jones

Martha's mum

Francine Jones
Martha's mum

Francine is Martha's mum. She is separated from Martha's dad Clive but has a good relationship with her three children – Tish is her eldest daughter, Martha is in the middle and her youngest is Leo. Francine finds her ex-husband difficult – and she manages to insult Clive's new girlfriend at a party for Leo's 21st birthday on the day Martha went to the Moon and back. It is at the Lazarus party the following night that a man warns Francine about Martha's new friend, which concerns her – she even slaps the Doctor. The same week, a sinister woman listens in on a telephone call between her and Martha. She is eventually arrested along with her ex-husband and Tish, and she is forced to work as one of the Master's servants – until Martha saves her and the rest of the world.

Statistics

DEBUT	*Smith and Jones* (2007)
PLAYED BY	Adjoa Andoh
HOME	London, England
STATUS	Friend
HEIGHT	1.58m
SCARE RATING	[1] Not applicable — but she has a quick temper
SPECIAL FEATURES	[1] Not applicable
WEAPONS	[2] None, although she pointed a gun at the Master
LIKES	Her children
DISLIKES	Harold Saxon, the Master, the Doctor
TALK	'I don't like what's been happening with that Doctor. I don't think you're safe.'

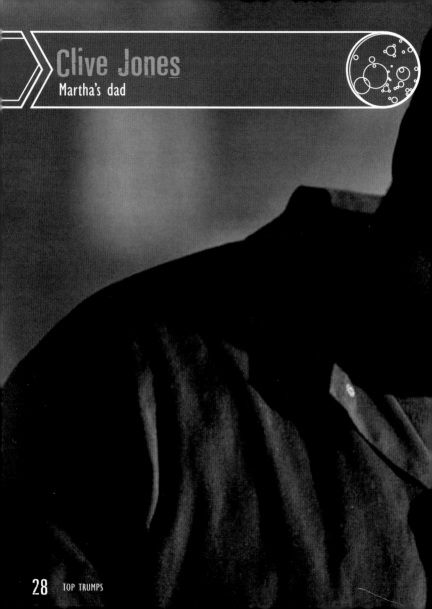

Clive Jones
Martha's dad

Clive Jones is Martha's dad. He is a successful businessman. However, Clive appears to be having a mid-life crisis, driving around in a sports car with a girlfriend called Annalise, who is around the same age as Martha. Tish, Leo and Martha all adore him and are always concerned for Clive when he meets up with Francine, as a fight usually follows. As part of the Master's trap, Clive and Francine are encouraged by a sinister woman to lure Martha back home. Francine pretends that she is thinking of getting back together with her ex-husband in the hope that Martha might come back. Martha immediately realises something is wrong – and asks her dad what is going on. Clive is brave enough to tell her to get away – leading to his arrest, along with Francine and Tish, and he spends a year working for the Master on board the Valiant.

Statistics

DEBUT	*Smith and Jones* (2007)
PLAYED BY	Trevor Laird
HOME	London, England
STATUS	Friend
HEIGHT	1.75m
SCARE RATING	[I] Not applicable
SPECIAL FEATURES	[I] None
WEAPONS	[I] None
LIKES	His family, Annalise
DISLIKES	People who voted for Harold Saxon, Francine's temper
TALK	'Just run, Martha, listen to me, just *run* — I don't know who they are, just run!'

Tish Jones
Martha's sister

Tish Jones
Martha's sister

Letitia Jones, known as Tish, is the eldest daughter of the Jones family. She is close to her sister Martha, and when she disappears with the Royal Hope Hospital she is concerned. Tish works as Head of PR for Lazlabs – but this is all part of a trap laid down by the Master. At first she finds Lazarus creepy until he transforms himself into a younger man. She flirts with Lazarus, not realising he is about to become a horrible creature! Martha warns her and she becomes annoyed, wondering why Martha always finds fault with anyone she meets. She later becomes an assistant to Prime Minister Harold Saxon and works at 10 Downing Street. It is not clear to Tish what her job involves, but Saxon doesn't care. She is arrested and taken aboard the Valiant, where she spends a year as a servant.

Statistics

DEBUT	*Smith and Jones (2007)*
PLAYED BY	Gugu Mbatha-Raw
HOME	London, England
STATUS	Friend
HEIGHT	1.63m
SCARE RATING	[1] Not applicable
SPECIAL FEATURES	[1] None
WEAPONS	[1] None
LIKES	Her family
DISLIKES	The Master, the Lazarus Creature
TALK	'Oh no, he's a science geek!'

Leo Jones
Martha's brother

Leo Jones
Martha's brother

Leo is the youngest member of the Jones family. He lives in London with his girlfriend Shonara and they have a baby called Keisha. His 21st birthday brings his whole family together, but the night ends abruptly when his mum insults his dad's girlfriend, Annalise – and the Jones family all storm out of the party. The Doctor watches this happening. The following night Leo suffers concussion at a party for Professor Lazarus' new machine, when the horrific Lazarus Creature flings a table at him and Francine. Later the same week he goes to Brighton with Shonara and Keisha and visits a friend called Boxer. By doing this he luckily manages to hide from the Master and evade capture. Leo and Martha are the only members of the Jones family that avoid serving the Master.

Statistics

DEBUT	*Smith and Jones* (2007)
PLAYED BY	Reggie Yates
HOME	London, England
STATUS	Friend
HEIGHT	1.75m
SCARE RATING	[I] Not applicable
SPECIAL FEATURES	[I] None
WEAPONS	[I] None
LIKES	Brighton, his girlfriend and daughter
DISLIKES	Annalise, concussion
TALK	'If anyone asks me to fetch them a drink, I'll swing for them.'

Empress of the Racnoss
Scary alien lady

Empress of the Racnoss

Scary alien lady

The Racnoss are a race of giant red alien creatures that scuttled around the universe in the Dark Times, billions of years ago. The Racnoss are always hungry and can eat whole planets – these monsters are born starving and need masses of food to survive. For a long time, it is thought that the Racnoss are all dead. However, back in the Dark Times some of them escaped, and planet Earth formed around a Webstar carrying Racnoss. They lie undisturbed inside the planet until their Empress, who is hiding at the edge of the universe, wakes up. The Empress wants to wake her hibernating children and allow them to feast on the Earth. However her plan to wake them using Huon particles and a new bride Donna fails when the Doctor appears. The army shoots down her giant Webstar spaceship when they receive orders from Harold Saxon.

Statistics

DEBUT	*The Runaway Bride* (2006)
PLAYED BY	Sarah Parish
HOME	Deep Space
STATUS	Scary alien lady
HEIGHT	4m
SCARE RATING	[8] Terrifying
SPECIAL FEATURES	[7] Teleportation
WEAPONS	[5] Energy bolts from Webstar, sticky web, Huon particles
LIKES	Lance Bennett, her children, shouting
DISLIKES	Water, the Doctor, Gallifrey
TALK	'Harvest the humans! Reduce them to meat.'

Lance Bennett
Traitor groom

Lance Bennett
Traitor groom

Lance Bennett is the Head of a Human Resources department for a company called H C Clements, a security firm in London that specialises in entry codes and ID cards. He meets Donna Noble while working there, takes an interest in her and makes coffee for her every day. Donna mistakes this for love. Lance is actually dosing Donna with Huon particles in the coffee which makes Donna an important part of a horrible plan to wake hibernating creatures. Donna pesters Lance to marry her – and he agrees, but only because he wants to keep her close to him so that he can hand her over to the Empress of the Racnoss. The Racnoss promises to show Lance the universe if he helps her. When the plan goes wrong and Donna escapes, the Empress uses Lance to wake her children instead – and he is thrown into the centre of the Earth.

Statistics

DEBUT	*The Runaway Bride* (2006)
PLAYED BY	Don Gilet
HOME	London, England
STATUS	Traitor
HEIGHT	1.70m
SCARE RATING	[4] His plans are scary
SPECIAL FEATURES	[1] Not applicable
WEAPONS	[1] His new best friend, the Empress of the Racnoss
LIKES	Racnoss, power
DISLIKES	Donna
TALK	'Months I had to put up with her. Months. A woman who can't even point to Germany on a map.'

Roboforms
Robot scavengers

Roboforms
Robot scavengers

The Roboforms are scavenging robots that scour the universe ahead of bigger and more dangerous threats. The first time the Doctor meets them, he is recovering from his difficult regeneration. The robots disguise themselves so they don't stand out – so when they arrive on Earth prior to the Sycorax invasion one Christmas, they adopt a festive disguise and look like Santa Clauses. As Rose and Mickey do some last-minute Christmas shopping, the Roboforms sense the energy from the Doctor's regeneration on Rose, and try to kill the pair by firing at them with their trombone flame-thrower weapons, and completely destroy a Christmas market. The Doctor runs into the Roboforms again the following Christmas – and this time they are being controlled by the Empress of the Racnoss, who uses the dangerous robots to track down Donna Noble and lead the bride into a deadly trap.

Statistics

DEBUT	*The Christmas Invasion* (2006)
PLAYED BY	Various
HOME	Unknown
STATUS	Scavenging enemy
HEIGHT	1.83m
SCARE RATING	[5] Sinister, silent and scary
SPECIAL FEATURES	[7] Disguise
WEAPONS	[7] Trombone flame throwers, exploding baubles, killer Christmas trees
LIKES	Christmas
DISLIKES	Sonic waves and the Doctor
TALK	Silent robots, although they can play musical instruments

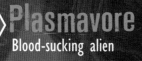

Plasmavore
Blood-sucking alien

Plasmavore
Blood-sucking alien

Florence Finnegan is not all she appears to be. She looks like a harmless old lady in her seventies, but she is actually a very dangerous criminal in hiding. 'Florence' is actually a disguised Plasmavore, who chooses to hide in the Royal Hope Hospital in London. A Plasmavore is an internal shape-changer that needs a constant supply of blood to stay alive – so a hospital is the perfect place to hide in. A Plasmavore is able to drink alien blood and change its internal chemistry to match that of the blood donor. In this way, the Plasmavore is able to escape the Judoon – until she drinks the Doctor's alien blood with her handy bendy straw, which she keeps in her handbag. The Judoon are looking for her because the Plasmavore murdered the Child Princess of Padrivole Regency Nine – and when they find her execute her immediately.

Statistics

DEBUT	*Smith and Jones* (2007)
PLAYED BY	Anne Reid
HOME	Unknown
STATUS	Bloodthirsty enemy
HEIGHT	1.68m
SCARE RATING	[7] Scary
SPECIAL FEATURES	[8] Can change internal biological make-up
WEAPONS	[7] A bendy straw
LIKES	Blood
DISLIKES	Judoon, child princesses
TALK	'Oh, I'm a survivor, Mr Stoker. At any cost.'

Slabs
Leather heavies

Slabs
Leather heavies

Slabs are basic slave
drones for alien
employers. Their whole
body is made of solid
leather, making the
Slabs incredibly tough
and strong. They are also
able to run very fast without
tiring. Martha first sees a Slab
outside her hospital, when one
knocks into her without apologising.
She mistakes it for a rude motorcycle
courier because while on Earth they
hide their true form underneath a black
motorcycle helmet. The Slabs work for
a Plasmavore, who likes to call them her
boys, and they carry out all her dirty work.
The Plasmavore uses the leather heavies
to pin down her victims while she drains
them of blood. The Doctor and Martha
manage to destroy one of them by
exposing it to a lethal dose of Roentgen
radiation – killing it dead. The Judoon
destroy the second Slab.

Statistics

DEBUT	*Smith and Jones* (2007)
PLAYED BY	Michael Williams, Matt Doman
HOME	Unknown
STATUS	Enemy helper
HEIGHT	1.90m
SCARE RATING	[6] Silent, sinister, scary
SPECIAL FEATURES	[4] Made of solid leather, speed
WEAPONS	[1] Tight grip
LIKES	Leather
DISLIKES	X-Ray departments and Roentgen radiation
TALK	Not applicable

Judoon
Interplanetary police for hire

Judoon
Interplanetary police for hire

The Judoon are a race of hulking creatures that work as hired police for whoever wants to pay enough money. The massive Judoon head has two fierce horns between a set of emotionless eyes. The Judoon space police dress in leather combat gear – big leather boots, thick leather skirt and a massive black helmet for protection. To help communicate they are able to adopt alien languages by scanning sounds, assimilating them, and plugging the scanning device into a nozzle on their chest. The Doctor and Martha meet the Judoon when the creatures use an H_2O scoop to remove a hospital from planet Earth and drop it on the Moon. According to Galactic Law the Judoon have no jurisdiction over the Earth, so they need to isolate the hospital in order to capture the Plasmavore who is hiding there.

Statistics

DEBUT	*Smith and Jones* (2007)
PLAYED BY	Various. Judoon Captain played by Paul Kasey. Voiced by Nicholas Briggs
HOME	Unknown
STATUS	Unintelligent thugs
HEIGHT	2m
SCARE RATING	[8] Scary
SPECIAL FEATURES	[7] Thick battle armour, language and species scanner
WEAPONS	[8] Blaster
LIKES	Stomping, justice, cataloguing
DISLIKES	Physical assault
TALK	'Justice is swift.'

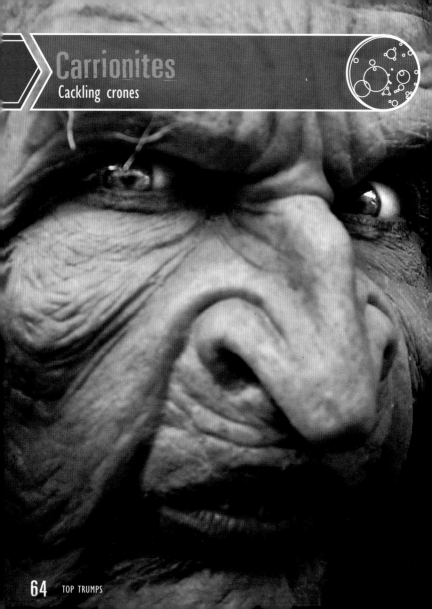

Carrionites
Cackling crones

Carrionites

Cackling crones

The Eternals banished the Carrionite race into Deep Darkness where they remained trapped forever. However, disappearing at the beginning of the universe, nobody was ever sure if the Carrionites were real or simply a legend. Carrionites use words and shapes as power. Three of them manage to escape due to the words of writer William Shakespeare. Mother Bloodtide, Mother Doomfinger and their young daughter Lilith plan to free the rest of their kind using more of Shakespeare's writing and bring about the Millennium of Blood. The horrible hags live in Allhallows Street and plot around a bubbling cauldron. They break the mind of architect Peter Streete, make him build the Globe Theatre to a special design and force Shakespeare to write a new play, *Love's Labour's Won*. The Doctor and Martha are able to stop the terrible plan just in time – and the escaping Carrionites are trapped inside a crystal ball.

Statistics

DEBUT	*The Shakespeare Code* (2007)
PLAYED BY	Christina Cole (Lilith), Amanda Lawrence (Doomfinger), Linda Clark (Bloodtide)
HOME	The Rexel Planetary Configuration
STATUS	Ruthless hunters
HEIGHT	Various
SCARE RATING	[8] Scary ladies
SPECIAL FEATURES	[8] Flight, physical transformation
WEAPONS	[6] Words, puppets, 'magic'
LIKES	Cackling, theatre, words, the works of Shakespeare
DISLIKES	Being named as Carrionites, being trapped, the Doctor
TALK	'At the Hour of Woven Words, we shall rise again, and this fleeting Earth will perish!'

William Shakespeare
Writer

William Shakespeare is the writer of many of the world's best-known plays and poems. His plays include *Macbeth, A Winter's Tale, A Midsummer Night's Dream* and *Love's Labour's Lost.* When the Doctor takes Martha on a trip back in time to 1599 they meet Shakespeare after seeing a performance of *Love's Labour's Lost* at the Globe Theatre, where he announces he is about to write a sequel to the play and that it will be performed the following night. The Doctor knows that this new play was only ever a rumour, so is interested to find out more. One of the Carrionites uses her power on Shakespeare to make him add special words to the new play – the combined power of writing and the Globe Theatre will release the trapped Carrionites. A clever man, Shakespeare is enchanted by Martha and thinks the Doctor and he are very alike. He lived from 1565 to 1616.

Statistics

DEBUT	*The Shakespeare Code* (2007)
PLAYED BY	Dean Lennox Kelly
HOME	London / Stratford-upon-Avon
STATUS	Genius, and very clever writer
HEIGHT	1.80m
SCARE RATING	[1] Not applicable, although his play *Macbeth* is scary
SPECIAL FEATURES	[8] Writing world-renowned plays
WEAPONS	[2] Not applicable, but his words are a weapon for the Carrionites
LIKES	Words, Martha, sonnets
DISLIKES	Sadness
TALK	'I must to work, I have a play to complete.'

Peter Streete
Unfortunate architect

Peter Streete
Unfortunate architect

Peter Streete is an architect who the
wicked Carrionites use in their plan to
set their sisters free. The horrible hags get
Peter to build the Globe Theatre in London
to their special design. It has 14 sides – a
tetradecagon – and he says it is designed like
that because it carries the sound well. What
he does not realise is that it is meant to play a
part in releasing the banished Carrionites. A month
after the Globe is finished being built, Peter ends up in
Bethlem Hospital, with his mind lost, talking about hearing
voices and witches. The Doctor, Martha and Shakespeare visit
him there to see what he knows. They discover a broken, scared
man. The Doctor hypnotises Peter to help him tell his story, but
before he can reveal too much, a Carrionite appears and kills him
with a deadly finger to the heart.

Statistics

DEBUT	*The Shakespeare Code* (2007)
PLAYED BY	Matt King
HOME	Bethlem Hospital
STATUS	Unfortunate architect
HEIGHT	1.75m
SCARE RATING	[1] Scared, rather than scary
SPECIAL FEATURES	[3] Good at designing theatres
WEAPONS	[1] Not applicable
LIKES	Architecture
DISLIKES	Witches and magic
TALK	'The witches spoke to Peter. In the night, they whispered...'

Macra
Snapping monsters

Macra
Snapping monsters

At the bottom of the Motorway
under New New York on New Earth
in the year five billion and fifty-three
there are beasts that the Doctor
encountered billions of years ago.
Massive crustaceans with big claws,
their bright eyes on stalks, they are
found piled up on top of each other
waiting to attack any passing vehicle.
Cars rarely survive the attacks. The
Macra used to be the scourge of
the galaxy, feeding off dirty gas – so
living amongst the car fumes of the
Motorway is perfect for them. In
the past they had a small empire and
used humans to mine for gas. When
the Doctor runs into them on New
Earth, they have devolved into simple
hungry beasts. Martha becomes
trapped in a car at the bottom
of the Motorway, along with her
kidnappers, Milo and Cheen, while
the Macra snap at their vehicle and
the Doctor tries to find her.

Statistics

MODERN DEBUT	*Gridlock* (2007)
PLAYED BY	Computer generated
HOME	New Earth
STATUS	Snap-happy monsters
HEIGHT	20m
SCARE RATING	[7] Horrific
SPECIAL FEATURES	[1] Size
WEAPONS	[3] None but their claws can tear metal
LIKES	Snapping at motorists, gas
DISLIKES	Cars, disturbance
TALK	'Snap!'

Novice Hame
Feline friend

Novice Hame
Feline friend

Novice Hame is a Sister of Plenitude, one of the Catkind nuns who once ran a hospital on New Earth in the far future. The Sisters make a lifelong vow to help others and heal the sick. To cure people, they used to breed humans deep beneath the hospital so they could infect them with all known diseases. When the Doctor first meets them he cures the patients and the New New York Police Department arrests the Sisters. Novice Hame is one of those arrested. When the Doctor meets Novice Hame on his return to New Earth, she explains how she sought forgiveness with the help of the Face of Boe, while he protected her from the virus that killed most of the inhabitants of New Earth. Novice Hame knows that the Face of Boe will speak one final secret and she is with him when he dies saving the planet.

Statistics

DEBUT	*New Earth* (2006)
PLAYED BY	Anna Hope
HOME	New Earth
STATUS	Reformed cat nun
HEIGHT	1.73m
SCARE RATING	[4] Only scary if you don't like cats
SPECIAL FEATURES	[5] Teleport device
WEAPONS	[3] Sharp claws, blaster
LIKES	Looking after the Face of Boe, the Goddess Santori, legends
DISLIKES	Viruses
TALK	'He protected me. And he has waited for you, these long years.'

The Face of Boe

Mysterious alien friend

The Face of Boe

Mysterious alien friend

The Face of Boe is a friendly alien that is a large head contained in a jar. Legends say that he has watched the universe grow old – and he has seen and heard many things. The Doctor first meets Boe on Platform One when the mysterious alien is the official sponsor for the event that watches the Earth explode in a ball of flames. Boe meets the Doctor again when he projects a psychic message across time asking the Time Lord to come to New Earth to visit him in hospital, where he is meant to be dying. The third and final time they meet, Boe's dying words to the Doctor are 'you are not alone' – implying that he is not the last Time Lord. The first letters of these four words spell out Yana – who is the Master's human form. The Face of Boe was also Captain Jack Harkness's nickname when he first became a Time Agent...

Statistics

DEBUT	*The End of the World* (2005)
PLAYED BY	Voiced by Struan Rodger
HOME	The Silver Devastation
STATUS	Very old friend
HEIGHT	1.5m
SCARE RATING	[3] Not applicable
SPECIAL FEATURES	[8] Telepathy, teleportation
WEAPONS	[2] Not applicable
LIKES	Keeping secrets
DISLIKES	Talking
TALK	'Everything has its time. You know that, Doctor. Better than most.'

Pharmacists
Rogue traders

The grubby pharmacists are found in
Pharmacytown in the drab Undercity
of New New York on the planet
New Earth. When the Doctor and
Martha arrive there, three of them
open for business and attempt to
sell patches of moods to the time
travellers. Business is tough, and
the pharmacists call out like ticket
touts, desperate to make a sale. The
moods, which include Angry, Mellow
and Happy are powerful patches
that work instantly. The Doctor and
Martha witness a girl buying a patch
called Forget, because her parents
have gone. It is in Pharmacytown that
Martha is kidnapped and taken onto
the Motorway. The Doctor is furious.
After the pharmacists tell him how
to get to the Motorway he tells
them to shut down their businesses
immediately. Returning that evening,
it appears that they have listened to
him, and their booths are all boarded
up and the pharmacists have gone.

Statistics

DEBUT	*Gridlock* (2007)
PLAYED BY	Tom Edden, Natasha Williams, Gayle Telfer Stevens
HOME	New Earth
STATUS	Rogue traders
HEIGHT	Various
SCARE RATING	[1] Not applicable, just grubby
SPECIAL FEATURES	[1] None
WEAPONS	[1] None — but certain moods can kill
LIKES	Selling mood patches
DISLIKES	The Doctor telling them what to do
TALK	'Used to be thriving, this place, you couldn't move. But they all go to the Motorway, in the end'

Thomas Kincade Brannigan
Kindly Human Cat

Thomas Kincade Brannigan is an old-fashioned Catkind, a roguish ginger tom who the Doctor meets on the Motorway under New New York. He likes to wear goggles, flying-helmet, a leather jacket and scarf. Brannigan spots the Doctor at a lay-by in Pharmacytown and invites him to join him and Valerie, who is human. The couple have been on the Motorway for twelve years – since they were newlyweds – yet they have only travelled five miles. They had heard there are jobs available on Fire Island, so they joined the Motorway at Battery Park and are heading there. Brannigan and Valerie have a small family of kittens – Children of the Motorway that are two months old. The Doctor tries to convince Brannigan to help him find Martha. Reluctant to risk his family's life, Brannigan refuses, and watches the Doctor leap down through the cars on the Motorway to search for his friend.

Statistics

DEBUT	*Gridlock* (2007)
PLAYED BY	Ardal O'Hanlon
HOME	New Earth
STATUS	Feline friend
HEIGHT	1.90m
SCARE RATING	[1] None, unless you're afraid of cats
SPECIAL FEATURES	[2] Dresses in flying gear
WEAPONS	[1] None
LIKES	Valerie, his children, teasing the Cassini sisters
DISLIKES	Being stuck on the Motorway
TALK	'Think you know us so well, Doctor. But we're not abandoned. Not while we have each other.'

Pig Slaves
Dalek experiments

The Pig Slaves are the cruel result
of Dalek experimentation. When
the Cult of Skaro find themselves in
1930s New York, they need a band
of slaves. As part of their master
plan, the Daleks take humans of low
intelligence and turn them into pig
creatures that are part human, part
animal. The Daleks then use them
to gather more humans for their
experiments by sending the Pig Slaves
into New York, making them bring
people down into the sewers beneath
Manhattan. They are aggressive and
savage creatures that lurk in the dark
sewers and they are trained to rip
throats with their bare teeth. The Pig
Slaves have a short life-span – most
of them live for only a few weeks.
One Pig Slave, Laszlo, manages to
escape, and is able to keep his own
mind. The Doctor is able to save him
using Dalek equipment.

Statistics

DEBUT	*Daleks in Manhattan* (2007)
PLAYED BY	Various, Laszlo played by Ryan Carnes
HOME	Earth
STATUS	Dangerous grunting pigs
HEIGHT	Various
SCARE RATING	[7] Scary
SPECIAL FEATURES	[5] Pig faces
WEAPONS	[3] None barring strength and sharp teeth
LIKES	Grunting, lifts, serving the Daleks
DISLIKES	Electricity
TALK	'Grunt.'

Solomon
Hooverville leader

Solomon
Hooverville leader

Solomon is the leader of Hooverville in New York's Central Park in 1930. He fought in the First World War and ends up in Hooverville during the height of the Depression, along with hundreds of other people who have nowhere else to go. Solomon cannot understand why the tallest building in the world – the Empire State Building – is being built while there are people starving in Manhattan. He joins the Doctor and Martha in their search for missing people of Hooverville and ends up in the Manhattan sewers avoiding Pig Slaves. Solomon is a brave man, and when the Daleks turn up at Hooverville looking for the Doctor he tries to reason with them, explaining to them that they are similar to the people of Hooverville, having no home, future or friends. He begs the Daleks for compassion, but they exterminate him without hesitation.

Statistics

DEBUT	*Daleks in Manhattan* (2007)
PLAYED BY	Hugh Quarshie
HOME	Earth
STATUS	Friend
HEIGHT	1.80m
SCARE RATING	[1] Not applicable
SPECIAL FEATURES	[3] Bravery
WEAPONS	[1] None
LIKES	Leading Hooverville
DISLIKES	Daleks
TALK	'Aren't we the same? Underneath it all, aren't we kin?'

HOOVER VILLE

Mr Diagoras
Unwilling Dalek slave

Mr Diagoras is a tough businessman who wants
to run New York. He is in charge of constructing
the Empire State Building. In 1930, it is going
to be the tallest building in the world. But Mr
Diagoras is working for the Daleks, who are
using him to lure people of Hooverville down
into the sewers. The people who go there
will never return, as they will become part
of the Dalek workforce. As part of their final
experiment, the Daleks need a special mast in
place at the top of the Empire State Building,
fitted with Dalekanium. Diagoras promises his
masters that he will complete the project on
time. One Dalek tells him that he thinks like
a Dalek, and when Dalek Sec orders Diagoras
to be brought to their transgenic lab in the
basement of the building, Dalek Sec uses him
for the survival of the Dalek race...

Statistics

DEBUT	*Daleks in Manhattan* (2007)
PLAYED BY	Eric Loren
HOME	Earth
STATUS	Treacherous businessman
HEIGHT	1.91m
SCARE RATING	[3] Scary, but his masters are scarier
SPECIAL FEATURES	[5] Thinks like a Dalek
WEAPONS	[1] None
LIKES	Power
DISLIKES	Dalek Sec
TALK	'I've been a soldier myself. And I swore then, I'd survive, no matter what.'

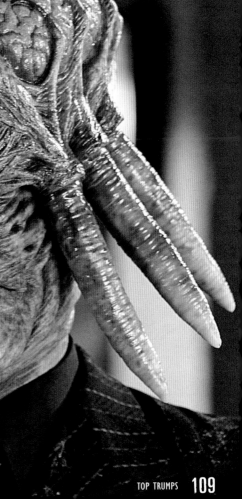

Dalek Sec Hybrid
Horrific hybrid creature

The Dalek Sec Hybrid is the hideous result of a Dalek experiment. The Cult of Skaro believe they are the only four Daleks in existence, and Dalek Sec is their leader. To save the Daleks, Sec sacrifices his Dalek form. He opens his casing and merges with an unwilling Mr Diagoras, trapping the man inside the Dalek casing. When the experiment is complete, Sec opens up again to reveal a new kind of creature – a revolting one-eyed monstrosity, with disgusting tentacles. He is the genetic template for a new race of Dalek-Humans. Feeling humanity is a different experience for a Dalek, and the Dalek Sec Hybrid begins to question everything that Daleks usually stand for. He feels sorry for the death of Hooverville leader, Solomon. The remaining Daleks see the Dalek Sec Hybrid as a threat to their existence. They chain him up and eventually exterminate him.

Statistics

DEBUT	*Daleks in Manhattan* (2007)
PLAYED BY	Eric Loren
HOME	Earth
STATUS	Enemy
HEIGHT	1.91m
SCARE RATING	[9] Terrifying
SPECIAL FEATURES	[4] One eye, part Dalek, part man, exposed brain
WEAPONS	[1] None
LIKES	Walking
DISLIKES	Eventually dislikes what it is to be a Dalek
TALK	'I am Human Dalek. I am your future!'

Tallulah
Showgirl

Tallulah is a dancer and singer who works at the Laurenzi, a theatre in New York in 1930. Her boyfriend, Laszlo, brings her a rose every day before her show. When Laszlo disappears, Tallulah is left wondering what has happened to him – although a rose continues to appear on her dressing-room table. Every night, Laszlo, who is now part-Pig Slave, watches Tallulah perform her show from the side of the stage, but he is afraid of her reaction and does not want her to see him looking like a pig. Tallulah heads into the sewers with the Doctor and together they meet Laszlo. Appalled at what the Daleks have done to him, she helps the time travellers with their fight against the alien threat. Along with Martha, she breaks into the Empire State Building and electrocutes the pursuing Pig Slaves.

Statistics

DEBUT	*Daleks in Manhattan* (2007)
PLAYED BY	Miranda Raison
HOME	Earth
STATUS	Dancing friend
HEIGHT	1.65m
SCARE RATING	[1] Not applicable
SPECIAL FEATURES	[4] Good singing voice
WEAPONS	[1] She has a gun, but it is only a theatre prop
LIKES	Entertaining, Laszlo
DISLIKES	Daleks
TALK	'If that's not a human being, that kinda implies... it's from outer space.'

Dalek-Humans
Dalek experiments

Dalek-Humans
Dalek experiments

Desperate to survive, the last four Daleks carry out experiments to keep their race alive. They create embryos – the Doctor finds one in the sewers of Manhattan – but these fail because the flesh is too weak. Dalek Sec merges with a human to create a genetic template for a new race of Daleks – Dalek-Humans. The Daleks kidnap more than a thousand humans and keep them near death with their minds wiped. Using the conductor at the top of the Empire State Building to power the experiment, Dalek Sec Hybrid's altered DNA is to be given to each human body and gamma radiation will waken the Dalek-Humans. The Doctor's DNA mixes with the Dalek-Humans by accident, so the new race of creatures begin to question and they shoot Daleks Jast and Thay. The last remaining Dalek, Dalek Caan, decides to destroy them all.

Statistics

DEBUT	*Evolution of the Daleks* (2007)
PLAYED BY	Various
HOME	Earth
STATUS	Empty humans
HEIGHT	Various
SCARE RATING	[7] Scary humans
SPECIAL FEATURES	[4] Look human, act like Daleks
WEAPONS	[5] Dalek guns
LIKES	Marching
DISLIKES	Dalek Caan
TALK	'But you are not — our Master. And we... we are not Daleks.'

Lazarus
Professor turned creature

Lazarus
Professor turned creature

Professor Richard Lazarus promises to change what it means to be human. And he certainly does. Lazarus, with the backing of Harold Saxon, creates a machine called a Genetic Manipulation Device, which is able to rejuvenate the human body. Lazarus steps into the machine aged 76 – and steps out looking as if he is in his 30s. Everything starts to go wrong when dormant genes in Lazarus's DNA reactivate something horrible that evolution rejected millions of years ago. The result is a massive monster – a creature that is hungry for the life energy of humans. His first victim is Lady Thaw, his business partner of many years. The creature ends up playing a deadly game of hide and seek with the Doctor and Martha, and eventually hides in Southwark Cathedral. Here the Lazarus Creature is disorientated when the Doctor magnifies the sonic resonance of the organ music and it falls to its death from the church bell tower.

Statistics

DEBUT	*The Lazarus Experiment* (2007)
PLAYED BY	Mark Gatiss and computer generated
HOME	Earth
STATUS	Vain professor / horrible creature
HEIGHT	Various
SCARE RATING	[8] Terrifying
SPECIAL FEATURES	[6] Lethal life-draining tail, expanding jaw, huge pincers
WEAPONS	[3] Hulking body
LIKES	Food, human energy
DISLIKES	Loud sounds
TALK	'I'm only doing what everyone before me has tried to do. I've simply been more successful.'

Lady Thaw
Unfortunate business partner

Lady Thaw
Unfortunate business partner

The wealthy Lady Sylvia Thaw is
Professor Richard Lazarus's business
partner at Lazarus Laboratories in
London. Driven by money, she is
concerned about the financial side of
the experiments if they are deemed
unsafe. The people invited to the
party are able to put in billions of
pounds worth of investment, after
all. She is also working with Harold
Saxon. On witnessing the successful
experiment she is determined to be
next in line for rejuvenation – like
Lazarus, she too is in her seventies.
However, the young-looking
Professor cruelly mocks her ideas
of ruling an empire from the success
of the experiments. Upset at her
partner's behaviour, she becomes
concerned when Lazarus starts
to spasm. Unsure what to do she
watches in horror as the Professor
turns into the huge creature. He
sucks the life out of her body and she
drops to the ground.

Statistics

DEBUT	*The Lazarus Experiment* (2007)
PLAYED BY	Thelma Barlow
HOME	Earth
STATUS	Corrupt businesswoman
HEIGHT	1.54m
SCARE RATING	[1] Not applicable
SPECIAL FEATURES	[2] Good with money
WEAPONS	[1] None
LIKES	Power
DISLIKES	Dangerous experiments
TALK	'I made you. You would be nothing if I hadn't backed you.'

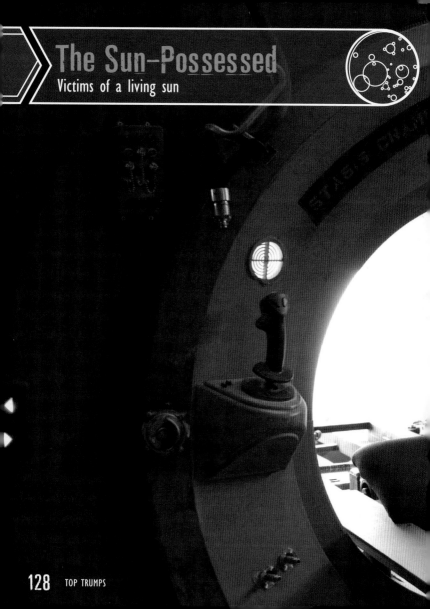

The Sun-Possessed
Victims of a living sun

When the TARDIS receives a distress signal and arrives aboard the SS *Pentallian*, there are only 42 minutes left until the ship crashes into a sun. The ship is working its way across the Torajii star system when it runs into trouble – the engines die without warning. Two of the crew, Korwin McDonnell and Dev Ashton, become infected by an alien force. Their body temperatures rise to over 100 degrees and they attempt to kill everyone aboard the ship. Burning light pours from their eyes as they attack the rest of the crew. The nearby sun is alive and it possesses and communicates with the Doctor. Unknowingly, the captain of the ship has taken part of it to use for fuel and now it is screaming for it to be returned. Martha helps the crew dump the fuel and the ship escapes destruction.

Statistics

DEBUT	42 (2007)
PLAYED BY	Matthew Chambers and Gary Powell
HOME	A living sun in the Torajii star system
STATUS	Sun-possessed humans
HEIGHT	Various
SCARE RATING	[9] Hot and scary
SPECIAL FEATURES	[7] Blinding light
WEAPONS	[7] Heat from their eyes
LIKES	Burning
DISLIKES	Cold, the crew of the SS Pentallian
TALK	'Burn with me.'

John Smith
The Doctor in disguise

When the Doctor is trying to hide his true identity, he sometimes goes by the name of John Smith. He uses it while he is in the Royal Hope Hospital, and introduces himself to Martha Jones as Mr Smith. However, when he is on the run from the Family of Blood, he gives up his Time Lord form and becomes an actual human called John Smith, using the TARDIS Chameleon Arch to hide his Time Lord self inside a innocent-looking fob watch. He is now completely human, with only one heart and working as a schoolmaster at Farringham School for Boys in Herefordshire. John Smith has the most amazing dreams. He dreams he has all sorts of adventures and meets all manner of strange creatures and people – he writes them all down in a form of fiction in a book he calls A Journal of Impossible Things. John Smith falls in love with a nurse at the school – but he isn't actually real.

Statistics

DEBUT	*Human Nature* (2007)
PLAYED BY	David Tennant
HOME	Farringham School for Boys, Herefordshire
STATUS	Friendly human
HEIGHT	1.85m
SCARE RATING	[1] Mostly harmless
SPECIAL FEATURES	[4] Has a pocket watch and keeps a dream journal
WEAPONS	[1] Only those provided by the school
LIKES	Dreaming, Joan Redfern
DISLIKES	The Family of Blood
TALK	'That's me. Completely human.'

The Family of Blood
Alien hunters

The Family of Blood

Alien hunters

The Family of Blood is a race of hunters with an ability to sniff out anyone they want. When the Family's life spans start to run out they want the Doctor and his Time Lord body to help their son live for a long time. The Family steal Time Agent technology and are able to track the Time Lord across time and space, so the Doctor becomes human and hides with Martha in a school in 1913, waiting for them to die. The Family travel across the universe looking for him until they land their invisible spaceship near the school. Father of Mine takes over a farmer called Clark, Mother of Mine takes over Martha's only real friend Jenny, Son of Mine uses schoolboy Jeremy Baines, and Daughter of Mine steals young Lucy Cartwright's form. But the Family can only live for three months so the race is on to find the Doctor.

Statistics

DEBUT	*Human Nature* (2007)
PLAYED BY	Gerard Horan, Rebekah Staton, Harry Lloyd, Lauren Wilson
HOME	Unknown
STATUS	Fearsome foes
HEIGHT	Various
SCARE RATING	[9] Terrifying
SPECIAL FEATURES	[9] Telepathy, body snatching, good sense of smell
WEAPONS	[7] Blasters and the scarecrows
LIKES	Sniffing, possessing people, Time Lords
DISLIKES	The Doctor's wrath
TALK	'He never raised his voice. That was the worst thing. The fury of the Time Lord.'

When the Family of Blood arrive in England, 1913, they need an army to help find the missing Doctor. Son of Mine creates hundreds of scarecrow soldiers with molecular fringe animation and they wait patiently to receive orders. These sinister scarecrows undertake some horrible tasks for the Family. They first attack a farmer called Mr Clark and drag him back to the Family's ship. They also grab a young girl and a maid from the school so that the aliens can inhabit their bodies too. When the Family discover that John Smith is the Doctor in disguise they use the scarecrows to attack the school. A vicious fight follows between the schoolboys and scarecrows – most of the straw men are ripped apart. Son of Mine reanimates them quickly enough and they find the TARDIS. When the Doctor captures the Family, the scarecrows have nothing to power them, and become ordinary scarecrows.

Statistics

DEBUT	*Human Nature* (2007)
PLAYED BY	Various
HOME	Not applicable
STATUS	Scary straw men
HEIGHT	Various
SCARE RATING	[9] Terrifying
SPECIAL FEATURES	[7] Lumbering and almost unstoppable
WEAPONS	[2] None
LIKES	Appearing at windows and being generally terrifying
DISLIKES	Bullets
TALK	Not applicable

Joan Redfern
School Matron

Nurse Joan Redfern is the school matron at Farringham School for Boys, the school where the Doctor and Martha are hiding from the Family of Blood in 1913. Her husband Oliver died at the Battle of Spion Kop. She finds the new schoolmaster, John Smith, quite extraordinary – and she bravely asks him out to a village dance. John shows Joan his strange journal of dreams, and although she thinks he is a little eccentric, she at first mistakes this for shyness. She believes the man John writes about in his journal is the man he would like to be. Joan falls in love with John and ignores Martha when she tries to convince her that he is an alien. When the Doctor becomes a Time Lord again he asks her if she would like to travel with him as his companion. She declines, upset she has lost John Smith forever.

Statistics

DEBUT	*Human Nature* (2007)
PLAYED BY	Jessica Hynes
HOME	Farringham School for Boys, Herefordshire
STATUS	Friend
HEIGHT	1.67m
SCARE RATING	[1] Not applicable
SPECIAL FEATURES	[4] School nurse
WEAPONS	[1] None
LIKES	John Smith, village dances
DISLIKES	The Doctor, the Family of Blood
TALK	'And "alien" means...? Not from abroad, I take it?'

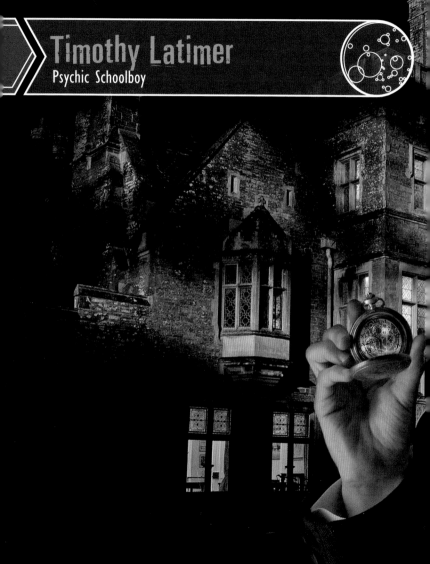

Timothy Latimer
Psychic Schoolboy

Timothy Latimer
Psychic Schoolboy

Timothy Latimer is psychic and is one of John Smith's pupils at the Farringham School. He is a quiet boy and is bullied by some of the other boys at the school – Hutchinson makes him do his Latin translations for him. Timothy sometimes says things that turn out to be correct. He is unable to explain why, but thinks it is luck, not realising he has an amazing talent. John Smith worries about Timothy and asks him to come to his study to borrow a book. He thinks that Timothy should be top of the class, but something is stopping him. While in John's study, Timothy finds the fob watch that contains the Doctor's Time Lord self. When he opens it the Family of Blood are alerted, and he has visions of monsters and also begins to see images of the Doctor and Martha in other times and places.

Statistics

DEBUT	*Human Nature* (2007)
PLAYED BY	Thomas Sangster
HOME	Boards at Farringham School
STATUS	Friend
HEIGHT	1.64m
SCARE RATING	[1] Not applicable
SPECIAL FEATURES	[8] Psychic
WEAPONS	[1] None
LIKES	John Smith, the Doctor
DISLIKES	Some of the other school boys, the Family of Blood
TALK	'I've seen him. And he's like fire. And ice. And rage. He's like the night and the storm and the heart of the sun...'

Weeping Angels
Lonely assassins

The Weeping Angels look like ancient stone statues, and look harmless enough at first. They are as old as the universe and used to be called the lonely assassins but no one knows where they come from. They cover their eyes because they cannot risk looking at each other. Their defence system is the most perfect ever evolved – they are quantum locked and don't exist when they are being observed. The moment a living creature sees one of them they freeze into rock without fail. However, if someone blinks or turns their back, the Weeping Angels are able to move. They kill people in a nice way though – one touch from a Weeping Angel will zap the victim into the past and let them live to death. They live on potential energy. When the Doctor and Martha are thrown back to 1969, they are concerned the Angels might feast off the energy inside the TARDIS next...

Statistics

DEBUT	*Blink* (2007)
PLAYED BY	Various
HOME	Unknown
STATUS	Lonely assassins
HEIGHT	Various
SCARE RATING	[9] The stuff of nightmares
SPECIAL FEATURES	[9] Quantum locked
WEAPONS	[6] Touch
LIKES	Potential energy
DISLIKES	Being seen
TALK	Not applicable

Sally Sparrow

The girl who saves the Doctor

Sally Sparrow is a pretty girl in her early twenties. She likes taking pictures of old things and because of this she breaks into the supposedly haunted Wester Drumlins House. While taking pictures she discovers a message from a man called the Doctor, written underneath old wallpaper, who seems to know her every move. Spooked by this, Sally returns to Wester Drumlins the following day with her friend Kathy, who disappears while they are looking around the house. As Sally soon discovers, there are Weeping Angel statues in the house that are waiting to zap unsuspecting people into the past. The Doctor, who has already been thrown back to 1969 with Martha, gets messages back to Sally through Easter eggs on her DVD collection in the hope she can return the TARDIS to him.

Statistics

DEBUT	*Blink* (2007)
PLAYED BY	Carey Mulligan
HOME	London
STATUS	Friend
HEIGHT	1.65m
SCARE RATING	[1] Not applicable
SPECIAL FEATURES	[3] Good photographer
WEAPONS	[1] None
LIKES	Billy Shipton, Larry Nightingale, solving puzzles, the Doctor
DISLIKES	Weeping Angels
TALK	'I'm clever and I'm listening. And don't patronise me because people have died and I'm not happy.'

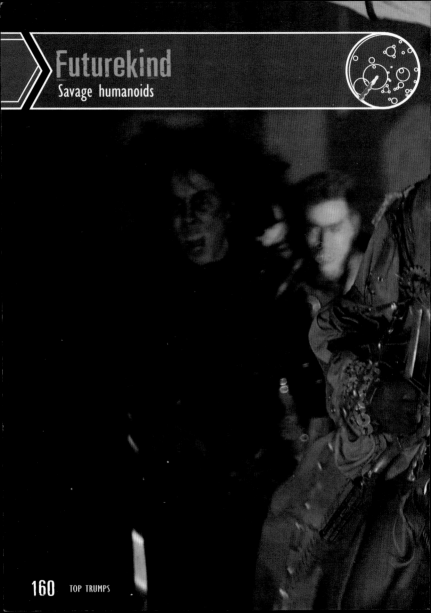

Futurekind

Savage humanoids

Futurekind

Savage humanoids

At the end of the universe there isn't much hope left for the human race. On the planet Malcassairo, a group of human survivors think that an old professor can get them off the planet and take them to Utopia. It is feared that if they remain there they will become like the wild hunting savages that run around in the wastelands – the humans call them the Futurekind. Ruled by an angry Chieftain, they have primitive speech patterns. Like animals, the Futurekind hunt out the human survivors on Malcassairo and feast on them. They can run incredibly fast and rip into human flesh with their jagged animal teeth. The Doctor, Martha and Jack manage to escape the Futurekind when they reach the safety of the Silo. But when the Master lowers the Silo's defences, the snarling barbarians break in.

Statistics

DEBUT	*Utopia* (2007)
PLAYED BY	Various
HOME	Malcassairo, at the end of the universe
STATUS	Angry humanoids
HEIGHT	Various
SCARE RATING	[8] Scary – run!
SPECIAL FEATURES	[6] Pointy teeth and wild looking
WEAPONS	[3] Primitive hunting tools
LIKES	Shouting, running
DISLIKES	Hunger, humans
TALK	'Humansss. Humansss are coming'

Professor Yana
A Time Lord in disguise

Professor Yana is an old man who is helping launch a rocket for the human race to get off the planet Malcassairo. The humans receive a signal to a place out towards the Wildlands and the Dark Matter Reefs. The message is simple: 'Come to Utopia.' Yana is using food to power the rocket but it isn't quite working – until the Doctor arrives. Years before, Yana was found abandoned on the coast of the Silver Devastation. He was a small orphan in a storm, with only one possession – a broken fob watch like the Doctor's. He has a constant drumming in his head and when he meets the Doctor and hears mention of time travel, Daleks and the Time War, the sound of drums increases. When Yana opens the watch his Time Lord self spills out and he becomes the Master and steals the Doctor's TARDIS.

Statistics

DEBUT	*Utopia* (2007)
PLAYED BY	Derek Jacobi
HOME	Found abandoned on the Silver Devastation
STATUS	Time Lord in disguise
HEIGHT	1.78m
SCARE RATING	[1] Not applicable
SPECIAL FEATURES	[5] Clever scientist
WEAPONS	[1] None
LIKES	Scientific research, hope
DISLIKES	The constant drumming in his head
TALK	'Those damn galaxies, they had to go and collapse!'

Chantho
The last of the Malmooth

Chantho
The last of the Malmooth

Chantho is a loyal, blue insectoid creature who works with Professor Yana on Malcassairo. It is thought that Chantho is the only survivor of the Malmooth, the original inhabitants of the planet before the humans arrived to take refuge. There is a vast city on the planet, but the conglomeration died for reasons unknown, yet somehow Chantho survived. She has assisted Yana for 17 years and loves the Professor deeply. Chantho is pleased to meet the Doctor, Martha and Jack. Jack flirts with her, which shy Chantho secretly enjoys. She also likes the company of Martha and she explains to her that she must start every sentence with 'Chan' and end every sentence with 'tho' – or it would appear she is swearing. Chantho witnesses Yana's transformation into the Master and the first thing he does is electrocute her. Before dying, Chantho is able to shoot him.

Statistics

DEBUT	*Utopia* (2007)
PLAYED BY	Chipo Chung
HOME	Malcassairo
STATUS	Friend
HEIGHT	1.65m
SCARE RATING	[1] Not applicable
SPECIAL FEATURES	[2] When talking, speech pattern
WEAPONS	[5] A blaster
LIKES	Professor Yana
DISLIKES	The Master
TALK	'Chan/it is said that I am the last of my species too/tho.'

The Master / Harold Saxon
A Time Lord reborn

Before they are destroyed, the Time Lords resurrect the long-dead Master because they know he is the perfect warrior for the Time War. He sees the Dalek Emperor take control of the Cruciform – but runs away because he is scared. He hides himself in human form as Yana, and it is many years before he opens the fob watch that contains his true Time Lord identity. When Chantho shoots him, he regenerates into a much younger man and steals the Doctor's TARDIS. The Doctor locks the TARDIS controls, so it can only travel between the last two destinations – the end of the universe and present-day Earth. On Earth, he calls himself Harold Saxon and sets up the Archangel network, allowing him to hypnotise the people of Earth and eventually become Prime Minster of Great Britain. But this is just the beginning of his diabolical plans.

Statistics

MODERN DEBUT	*Utopia* (2007)
PLAYED BY	Derek Jacobi, John Simm
HOME	Gallifrey
STATUS	Evil Time Lord
HEIGHT	Various
SCARE RATING	[9] Dangerous and scary
SPECIAL FEATURES	[9] Two hearts, ability to regenerate
WEAPONS	[8] Laser screwdriver
LIKES	Being lord and Master, power
DISLIKES	The Sound of Drums, the Doctor, humankind, the Daleks
TALK	'We meet at last, Doctor. Ooh, love saying that!'

Lucy Saxon
The Master's wife and faithful companion

Lucy is Harold Saxon's wife. She comes from a good family, went to a girls' school called Roedean, and she isn't particularly bright. Harold Saxon is kind to her father and Lucy soon falls for him. They marry before Saxon becomes Prime Minster of Great Britain. The Master promises her that no one will find out that Harold Saxon is fictitious – and she is upset when journalist Vivien Rook questions her about Saxon's sudden rise to leadership. The Master takes Lucy travelling to the future in the Doctor's TARDIS, and thinks of her as his faithful companion. The Master treats her incredibly badly – and leads her to turn against her husband after a year aboard the Valiant. She eventually shoots him, killing him in front of the Doctor. Later, the Doctor burns the Master's body on a funeral pyre.

Statistics

DEBUT	*The Sound of Drums* (2007)
PLAYED BY	Alexandra Moen
HOME	London, England
STATUS	Traitor
HEIGHT	1.70m
SCARE RATING	[1] Not applicable
SPECIAL FEATURES	[2] Faithful companion
WEAPONS	[1] None
LIKES	Power, Harold Saxon
DISLIKES	The Master
TALK	'The thing is... I made my choice. For better or for worse. Isn't that right, Harry?'

Tom Milligan
Freedom fighter

Tom Milligan
Freedom fighter

Tom Milligan is a doctor who used to work in paediatrics before the Master arrived on Earth and sent the Toclafane to kill. He is with the Peripatetic Medical Squad, which allows him to travel freely, so he becomes a freedom fighter. Tom meets Martha after she has been travelling the Earth for a year. They hit it off immediately, and Martha finds it ironic that she is travelling with a doctor again. Martha wants Tom to take her to Professor Docherty, who she knows will lead her back to the Master. While hiding in slave quarters in Bexley, the Master tracks Martha and Tom down – and shoots Tom with his laser screwdriver as he tries to protect her. When time returns to normal and the Earth goes back one year, Martha telephones the unharmed Tom at his hospital and she's happy to find that he is alive and well.

Statistics

DEBUT	*Last of the Time Lords* (2007)
PLAYED BY	Tom Ellis
HOME	London, England
STATUS	Friendly freedom fighter
HEIGHT	1.90m
SCARE RATING	[1] Not applicable
SPECIAL FEATURES	[2] Medically trained
WEAPONS	[1] Gun
LIKES	Martha
DISLIKES	Harold Saxon
TALK	'Lot of people depending on you. You're a bit of a legend.'

Toclafane
Danger from the future

Toclafane
Danger from the future

'Toclafane' is a made-up name from Gallifreyan fairytales. The Master uses the word to hide what the menacing silver spheres really are – the last six billion humans from the end of the universe. Leaving in the rocket from Malcassairo, the humans find nothing but the dark and cold. So they cannibalise themselves and regress into a childish state – putting themselves inside spheres – and share each other's memories. When the Master and Lucy arrive in Utopia he tells them he will rescue them and take them back to the 21st century. He links the Doctor's TARDIS into a Paradox Machine to allow the humans back to the Earth they once walked on – letting the future and the past collide with each other and change the history of the entire universe. Captain Jack destroys the Paradox Machine in the TARDIS and time turns back to before the six billion spheres invaded Earth.

Statistics

DEBUT	*The Sound of Drums* (2007)
PLAYED BY	Computer generated. Voiced by Zoe Thorne, Gerard Logan and Johnnie Lyne-Pirkis
HOME	The end of the universe and present-day Earth
STATUS	Deadly
HEIGHT	0.40m diameter
SCARE RATING	[8] Terrifying
SPECIAL FEATURES	[8] Teleportation, shared memories
WEAPONS	[9] Blades, fire bolts
LIKES	Playing, humour, the Master, paradoxes
DISLIKES	The cold and dark
TALK	'We come to build! A new Empire! Lasting a hundred trillion years!'

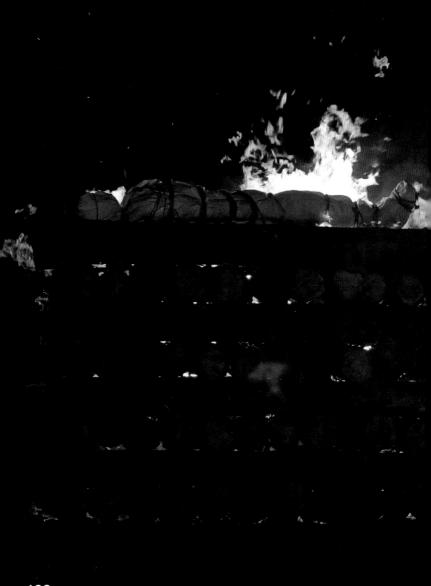

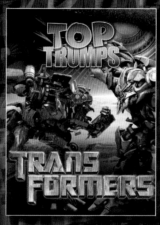

Great new Top Trumps packs
OUT NOW!

CLASSICS Dinosaurs • Ultimate Military Jets • Skyscrapers • The Dog
• World Football Stars • Wonders of the World • British Army Fighting Forces
• Wildlife in Danger

SPECIALS Roald Dahl • Star Wars 1-3 • Star Wars 4-6 • Star Wars
Starships • Star Wars Clone Wars • Horror • High School Musical
• Pirates of the Caribbean • Dr Who 2 • The Simpsons Classic Volume 1
• The Simpsons Classic Volume 2 • Bratz Passion for Fashion • WWE2
• Jacqueline Wilson • Transformers • Marvel Max • Harry Potter and the
Order of the Phoenix • Top Gear • DC Super Heroes • DC Super Heroes 2

SPORTS Newcastle FC • Tottenham Hotspur FC • Chelsea FC
• Man United FC • Arsenal FC • Liverpool FC • Football Legends

Play Top Trumps at
TOPTRUMPS.COM